The Healing Path

The Healing Path

A 30-Day Guide to Walking Healed
And Living in Freedom

Shelley Wilburn

The Healing Path
Copyright © 2019 Shelley Wilburn
Second edition, 2022

All rights reserved. No part of this publication may be reproduced, stored in a retrieval system, or transmitted in any form or by any means, electronic, mechanical, photocopying, recording or otherwise without the prior written permission of the author. Reviewers may quote briefly for review purposes.

All Scripture quotations, unless otherwise indicated, are taken from the Holy Bible, New Living Translation (NLT), copyright © 1996. Used by permission of Tyndale House Publishers, Inc. Carol Stream, IL USA. All rights reserved.

Scripture quotations marked NKJV are taken from the New King James version. Copyright © 1982. Used by Thomas Nelson Inc. Used by permission. All rights reserved.

The ESV® Bible (The Holy Bible, English Standard Version®). ESV® Text Edition: 2016. Copyright © 2001 by Crossway, a publishing ministry of Good News Publishers. The ESV® text has been reproduced in cooperation with and by permission of Good News Publishers. Unauthorized reproduction of this publication is prohibited. All rights reserved.

Scripture quotations marked ABOT are taken from the Amplified Bible, Old Testament. Copyright © 1965, 1987 by the Zondervan Corporation. Used by permission. All rights reserved.

Scripture quotations marked ABNT are taken from the Amplified Bible, New Testament. Copyright © 1954, 1958, 1987 by the Lockman Foundation. Used by permission.

The Voice Bible Copyright © 2012 Thomas Nelson, Inc. The Voice ™ translation © 2012 Ecclesia Bible Society All rights reserved.

>   Cover art by Paul Ruane
>   Edited by Rachel Wilburn
>   Published by Mismatched Socks Publishing
>   Walking Healed Ministries, LTD
>   ISBN 978-0-9864311-4-2
>   Library of Congress Control Number 2019909544

Table of Contents

Special Thank You i
Introduction iv
Day 1 Finding the Path 1
Day 2 You Are Healed 3
Day 3 Fear is a Liar 5
Day 4 The Right Path 7
Day 5 Pathway to Peace 9
Day 6 Rock of Refuge 12
Day 7 Lighting Up the Path 14
Day 8 One-Way Path 16
Day 9 Dress for the Weather 19
Day 10 Yesterday 21
Day 11 Detour on the Path 24
Day 12 Do It Afraid 26
Day 13 Get Grounded and Move Forward 28
Day 14 Walking in the Fog 31
Day 15 Play in the Rain 34
Day 16 Frustration on the Path 36

Day 17 Come Out of the Cave 38
Day 18 A Fork in the Path 40
Day 19 Don't Look Back! 43
Day 20 Setbacks, Struggles, and Stress 46
Day 21 Focus! 49
Day 22 When the Waters Rise 51
Day 23 Encouragement Along the Path 53
Day 24 Running on the Path 56
Day 25 Stuck in a Rut 59
Day 26 Get Up! 62
Day 27 Rescue on the Path 65
Day 28 Far Out! 68
Day 29 Truth is Greater than Fact 71
Day 30 Continue the Journey 74
About the Author 76
About Walking Healed Ministries LTD 78
Other Books by Shelley Wilburn 81

Special Thank You

This devotional was a surprise to me. You can laugh. I did. It's sort of a long story, but I'll give you the highlighted version to save time and space.

When I began revamping my blog, I nearly lost it all with one click of a button. In my panic and distress over thinking I lost over (at the time) six years' worth of writing, some sisters from church put me in contact with this guy named, Harold McGhee. They said he could help me. That was an understatement!

Harold came in, took my login information and passwords and said, "I'll get back to you." I really, really had to trust the Lord on this one, and Harold. Neither of them disappointed. In a matter of weeks I had a new website, a new ministry website, a new email location, a new, beautiful logo, and they were all my favorite colors! But it didn't stop there.

Harold also gave me an itinerary and a to-do list; one of them was to write a devotional. I thought I had other plans. Apparently not. Of course, I procrastinated, hesitated, grumbled, and I probably complained, but here it is. Finally!

Therefore, thank you, Harold McGhee, and

McGhee Enterprises, for pushing me and for not getting tired of my incessant questions. You are a tremendous asset to Walking Healed Ministries!

I also enlisted help in writing some of the devotions within this book. Special thanks to my dearest sisters Laurie Groves, Kerri Taylor, and Brenda West (my spiritual mother), for contributing to this project. Also thank you for believing in the vision God has given me. You help me continue the journey.

A very special thank you to my best-good-friend-ever-on-this-earth, my husband, Don (D.A.). You always understand. You always support me. You believe in me. But you also believe in the vision and calling God has on my life... because you are also part of that.

I also want to thank my daughter, Rachel, my firstborn, for editing this book. I love you more with each passing day. You will never know just how special you are to me. See, I told you that English Lit degree would come in handy!

To one of my favorite people, who happens to be my author coach, editor, favorite author, and best friend, Lisa Lickel. You get me out of so many jams! Thank you, my friend, for always being there.

And though this is the last, it's by far the most important: Thank You, Lord Jesus! Without You, none of this would be possible. Thank You for saving me. Thank You for healing me. Thank You for calling me into this ministry and for always walking with me on this journey on the Healing Path! I love you so much! May You get *all* the glory in every word I write and speak.

Introduction

Welcome to the Healing Path! The next thirty days are going to be an exciting journey. Beloved, healing is as close as your next step. Truly!

Follow this path and I'm confident you will find some amazing things that you may not have known. Or, maybe you knew them, but throughout the years, you've forgotten. Either way, may the Holy Spirit enlighten you afresh, making your walk on the healing path an enjoyable and blessed one.

At the end of each days' devotion, you will find Lights for Your Path. These are extra Scripture readings to help illuminate the path. Take a few minutes each day to look them up and read them. Use your favorite Bible translation. Read them out loud, because in doing so, you are declaring God's promises over your life. You are literally turning on lights, thereby lighting up the path ahead of you and making it clearer to see where you're going.

Let me tell you a little secret about reading (speaking) God's Word out loud:

The power of the Word is unleashed, turned loose, when you speak it out of your mouth. The more you do it, the stronger you get.

As you step out onto the Healing Path, many people will be walking with you. This devotional has been saturated in prayer, beloved. You are covered. You are welcomed onto the path. You even have a Guard in the Holy Spirit, who walks alongside you – as the LORD goes before you, and even behind you as your Rear Guard (Isaiah 52:12). You, precious one, are completely SAFE (Psalm 91) on this path.

Why thirty days? Because it takes twenty-one (21) days to make a new habit. Therefore, by Day Thirty you will be "rooted and grounded" in the Word and will crave your daily time with Him.

It is my sincerest prayer that each step you take over the next thirty days brings you not only closer to healing, but also closer to Jesus.

Day 1

Finding the Path

Thus says the Lord: "Stand by the roads, and look, and ask for the ancient paths, where the good way is; and walk in it, and find rest for your souls."
~Jeremiah 6:16a (ESV)

In the *Wizard of Oz*, Dorothy just wanted to find her way home. But she was in a foreign, albeit strange land. How could she know which way to go? How does one know where to find the path to healing?

Many people take many different paths, in search of that one miracle, that cure to all diseases. Some claim to have found it while others still search, valiantly. But what if the cure to all diseases is the same? What if, like eternal life, there is only one cure? There is.

His name is Jesus.

In John 14, Jesus is talking with His disciples, telling them He is getting ready to go to the Father (this is prior to His crucifixion). He tells them that when it is time, He will come back and get them so they can be with Him. Thomas stands up and asks how they can know the way to where He is going. Jesus, in His loving way, tells Thomas, "I am the way, the truth, and the life. No one can come to the Father except through me" John 14:6.

Jesus is the only way to Heaven. Likewise, Jesus is also the Cure to all our issues and diseases.

"Let all that I am praise the LORD; may I never forget the good things he does for me. He forgives all my sins and heals all my diseases," Psalm 103:2-3.

You don't have to follow the yellow brick road, or wear ruby red slippers. Nor do you have to click your heals three times to find the healing path. No, beloved. You're already on it.

Lights for Your Path

Psalm 103:2-3
John 14:6
Psalm 1:6
Proverbs 3:6

Day 2
You Are Healed

By His stripes you are healed. ~1 Peter 2:24b

It's difficult to comprehend, but we are actually, truly healed; from everything. God's Word declares it, not only in the Old Testament, but again in the New Testament. It doesn't say we will be healed. It says we are healed. What a way to begin this day. Stating the obvious, yet most difficult, statement to live by. We are healed.

So, how do you walk healed if you are experiencing mental, emotional, or physical issues? It's a matter of trusting God and taking Him at His word. Simply put, declaring it over yourself every single day.

I overheard a prominent preacher say something like this in one of his daily programs: "You have to speak healing over yourself every day. Make it a habit. Then one day, you will be going about your daily routine and suddenly notice that that issue is no longer an issue."

What is it that bothers you today? Is it anxiety, depression, an illness? Is there an issue which threatens to take over your life? Begin today with this declaration: "Lord, by your stripes, I AM healed! Thank you for healing me! No weapon formed against me will prosper because I am the head and not the tail, I am above and not beneath, and I am blessed! I am blessed coming in and blessed going out, and ALL of Your promises for me are "Yes!" and "Amen!" In Jesus' name, AMEN!"

Today is the beginning of a new day and a new path. The Healing Path!

Lights for Your Path

Isaiah 53:5
1 Peter 2:24
Isaiah 54:17

Day 3
Fear is a Liar

For God has not given us a spirit of fear, but of power and of love and of a sound mind. ~ 2 Timothy 1:7 (NKJV)

Many people struggle with stepping out into a new adventure because of fear. If we're afraid, we won't move. It's just easier to stay put and stay comfortable.

But God doesn't call us to stay in our comfort zone. He calls us out and up onto a higher plane. Then where does fear come from?

There's an old acronym which describes fear perfectly:

False Evidence Appearing Real.

Fear is false. It's a false emotion, ministered by the enemy of our souls (the devil), and magnified by our own insecurities to keep us from moving forward and living an abundant life.

Fear comes from the devil. The devil is a liar. Therefore, fear itself is a liar.

How long have you been lied to? How long have you desired to do that one thing that just the thought of it gives you an excitement deep within? How long have you suppressed it, because even though the thought is exciting, the fear of actually stepping out feels like a great weight?

It's time to throw off the weight of fear. Even though it seems heavy, it is not. It's an illusion. A spirit of heaviness. It's nothing but a lie.

Today is the day to put on a robe of righteousness, square your shoulders, hold your head up, smile, and step forward in boldness and confidence. The LORD is with you, dear one!

Lights for Your Path

Romans 8:15
Hebrews 12:1
Proverbs 20:10
Psalm 34:4

Day 4
The Right Path

There is a way that seems right to a man, But its end is the way of death. ~Proverbs 14:12 (NKJV)

The world has many pathways. Everyone seems to know which way is right. But God's Word has a different view of that.

When you've lived a certain way for so long, it can be a bit intimidating starting a new path. Of course, many begin and never finish, instead going back to what's familiar. As you embark on this journey on the Healing Path, remember that many will try to instruct you on the right way to go. Many will be wrong.

When it comes down to it, there is really only one right way. His name is Jesus. Therefore, as you step out onto the path, if you struggle with knowing which way is right, look to Jesus. He will never point you in the wrong direction. In fact, not only will He walk with you, but He has already gone before you and prepared the path for you. He will also be your rear guard, protecting you from behind. You can't lose, beloved.

Put one foot in front of the other and step forward. You are on the right path. Keep going. Ever forward.

Lights for Your Path

John 14:6
Isaiah 52:12

Day 5
Pathway to Peace

You will keep him in perfect peace whose mind is stayed on You, because he trusts in You. Trust in the Lord forever, for in Yah, the Lord, is everlasting strength. ~Isaiah 26:3-4 (NKJV)

Walking along a path, you must keep your mind focused on every step. You trust the path because you can see where you're going, yet you must watch where you step so you don't trip and fall. It's easy to get distracted with the scenery, things around you, people and activities. However, when we pay attention to where we are going, we find ourselves enjoying a peaceful walk. We can be confident to continue moving forward, not only in peace, but double the peace. How can that be?

When we keep our minds stayed, focused on what we are doing, we are less likely to be surprised by something or someone along the path. Have you ever been walking along and suddenly notice a movement at your feet, only to be surprised, or frightened, by a squirrel, a rabbit, or even a snake, darting from the underbrush? That's enough to cause your heart to pound.

It's the same with walking life's path. If we don't pay attention, it's easy for the enemy to sneak in and catch us unaware with various obstacles; financial, family, health, job issues, etc. But when we keep our focus on Jesus, though life happens, we won't find ourselves under intense stress, strain or worry. Instead, though we go through trying times, we can also get through them with peace.

Yah, the Lord, wants to double our peace and calmness. Each step you take on the path, is letting Him know you are trusting Him. In return, He will increase your strength, because He is our eternal strength.

The next time you begin to feel yourself tensing up, remember to adjust your focus. Stay your mind on Yah (short for Yahweh), the Lord. Trust Him. Focus on Him. Then allow Him to fill you with peace and strength.

Lights for Your Path

Matthew 6:33
John 16:33
2 Thessalonians 3:16
John 14:27
Colossians 3:15

Day 6
Rock of Refuge

In You, O LORD, I put my trust; Let me never be ashamed; Deliver me in Your righteousness. Bow down Your ear to me, Deliver me speedily; Be my rock of refuge, A fortress of defense to save me.
~Psalm 31:1-2 (NKJV)

If you have ever gone on a hike, or a walk through the woods, you know it can sometimes be a bit tedious; especially if there are obstacles (twigs, roots, rocks, etc.) on the path.

We can also attribute this to our life journey.

However, when we put our trust in the Lord, we never have to worry about things we may encounter along our path.

God walks with us, always listening, not only to us but to everything going on around us. He (our Rock), in His perfect ways, keeps us protected.

Like a gentle parent, He bends down to give us His attention, while also surrounding us (a fortress) keeping us safe from whatever would come at us.

And just as we may pause on a hike to rest upon a rock, to catch our breath, take a look around, or to take refuge, we can have the assurance that before we move on, we can also rest upon and be protected by God, our Fortress, our Rock of Refuge.

Lights for Your Path

Psalm 91:2
Psalm 46:1
Psalm 46:7

Day 7
Lighting Up the Path

You are the light of the world. A city that is set on a hill cannot be hidden. Nor do they light a lamp and put it under a basket, but on a lampstand, and it gives light to all who are in the house. Let your light so shine before men, that they may see your good works and glorify your Father in heaven. ~Matthew 5:14-16 (NKJV)

Jesus says we are the light of the world. If that's the case, how do we shed light on this path we are on?

Simple.

We walk on, being ourselves, loving others and ourselves. We put Jesus first in our lives, allowing Him to shine from every crack in us.

By putting Christ first in our lives, we allow Him to work through us. This gives an avenue to the Light which will begin to pour out into everything we do.

You know, the opposite of light is not dark.

Darkness is merely the absence of light. Therefore, on this path we walk, because of the light within you, YOU are the one lighting up the path. You do it by carrying the Word of God in you.

When you do, you're lighting up the way for others to follow. So shine, beloved!

Lights for Your Path

Matthew 5:16
Ephesians 5:8
Luke 11:36

Day 8
One-Way Path

Therefore, if anyone is in Christ, he is a new creation; old things have passed away; behold, all things have become new. ~2 Corinthians 5:17 (NKJV)

The Healing Path is a very unique path to walk. Once you're on it, it's important to keep moving forward. Being healed, saved, or even delivered, you have been made new; you're whole. Everything about you is changed.

Old things, the old way of life is gone; hence, your journey on the healing path.

Whatever you have been through, don't hide. Don't let what happened in the past dim your light. Don't put the lampshade on to shadow the light. Remove the lampshade and let the light within you shine bright. Put your focus on Jesus, the brightest light, and let Him lead you on the path.

By putting Christ first in our lives, we allow Him to work through us. This gives an avenue to the Light which will begin to pour out into everything. He will not only light up the path, but the area all around you. Let's face it, we are cracked vessels. We have brokenness from whatever we have been through in our lives that caused us pain. From depression, anxiety, intimidation, illness, abuse, discomfort, or whatever we've been through; we have cracks. But that's okay. God uses the broken, the cracked, the used and abused. He mends and heals, so that we can go out and shine.

You will not walk in darkness. You're on a brand-new path; One that is lit up with the light shining from within you.

If your old life, your old persona, is gone, you have no reason to turn back on the path. Besides, there are others coming after you who need the lights to guide them in the direction they need to go. Plus, it will be new to them as well.

You're not who you used to be, beloved. You have no business going back to the places you used to go. Don't go backwards. Become the light illuminates up the path for others to see the way to go.

Lights for Your Path

Lamentations 3:23
Ephesians 4:21-24

Day 9
Dress for the Weather

Laurie Groves

The land you have given me is a pleasant land. What a wonderful inheritance! I will bless the Lord who guides me; even at night my heart instructs me. I know the Lord is always with me. I will not be shaken, for he is right beside me. No wonder my heart is glad, and I rejoice. My body rests in safety. ~Psalm 16:6-9

Sometimes, our weather doesn't do what it should. For instance, when it's October and it should be cold outside, but instead we experience highs in the 80's and 90's every day.

One morning, God was speaking to me about how easy it is to resist a season you're in. It's especially easy when the season doesn't look or feel like you thought it would.

Every day we have this amazing choice: Embrace where you are or resist where you are.

Enjoy where you are or resent where you are.

My choice?

I'm going to dress for the weather. I'm going to embrace and enjoy the mess and the mundane.

I'm going to stop wasting precious energy on resisting and resenting the season I find myself in.

I'm going to speak life-giving words to myself. To the people around me. To my present and to my future!

Lights for Your Path

Proverbs 4:14
1 Peter 3:15
Proverbs 3:11
2 Timothy 2:21

Day 10

Yesterday

No, dear brothers and sisters, I have not achieved it (spiritual maturity), but I focus on this one thing: Forgetting the past and looking forward to what lies ahead, I press on to reach the end of the race and receive the heavenly prize for which God, through Christ Jesus, is calling us.
~Philippians 3:13-14 (emphasis added)

A few years ago I did a writing challenge from the website of a friend of mine. It was a weekly challenge to get the creative juices flowing. On one particular challenge we were to write something beginning with the letter "Y." It was harder than it sounds, but I finally decided on the word: Yesterday.

A lovely little rock band in the sixties once did a song expressing their desire for yesterday. Apparently to stay in yesterday all their troubles seemed far away. However, today it seemed as though they, the troubles, were here to stay. Therefore, it was just easier to believe in yesterday.

On our life's journey, it's very tempting, and often easy, to look back on yesterday. Yet, in doing so we aren't watching where we are going. It becomes even easier to stumble over things ahead in our path. There are some things in my own yesterday which I would simply like to forget. There are other things I would love to hold onto forever; my wedding day, my babies' first words and steps, goofy times I've had with each of my kids, even the birth of each of my grandbabies. It's a good thing we took pictures.

I guess it's good to remember the good things, but we also need to remember to let go of the yesterdays that were not so good. We need to focus on what lies ahead on our path, because it can only get better.

Life isn't perfect. But as an athlete practices and works for his goal, at the end of the race he is called forward to receive his prize. For us, if we stay focused forward, on Jesus, one day we will be called forward to receive our prize, too.

Lights for Your Path

1 Corinthians 9:24-25
2 Timothy 4:8
Romans 5:4
Matthew 6:21

Day 11

Detour on the Path

And your ears shall hear a word behind you, saying, "This is the way, walk in it," when you turn to the right or when you turn to the left. ~ Isaiah 30:21 (ESV)

On February 29th, 2012, I started writing in a journal. When I began, it was because everywhere I turned, there was a song, a commercial on TV, a devotion, or something that mentioned forgiveness. It dawned on me that the Lord might just be tapping me on the shoulder wanting me to pay attention. Therefore, I began writing about it. I thought, you know, that might come in handy one day. I might just need to write a book.

But, you see, timing is everything, and it's God's timing that needs to be kept. I didn't get around to actually writing until May, when my healing took place and God opened the gates for me to walk through on a new, healing path.

The enemy will set up road blocks along your

journey. He will cause you to take detours that you didn't intend to take. But if you'll read the Map (the Bible), and ask for directions, you'll have less road blocks and less detours. Back when I wanted to write but couldn't, I had not asked for directions and had actually put my Map down. I decided I could walk this path on my own. Big mistake!

Know this: you have things in your life, too. Little things. Things you have pushed to the far, dark corners of your mind. Things you don't want to deal with. Things that didn't seem important. However, they are important. If they are preventing you from continuing the walk on your path, they're important enough to be dealt with.

Right now, bring them out and let the Lord handle them for you. You may need to call in some Godly people who can pray with you. That's okay. That's what we're supposed to do; pray for each other.

Are you ready to continue on the path?

Lights for Your Path

James 5:13-15(a)
Hebrews 10:24
Proverbs 2:13
Job 28:23

Day 12
Do It Afraid

The fear of the Lord is the beginning of wisdom.
~ Psalm 111:10 (NKJV)

For years I feared the Lord. I thought He was this huge ruler, sitting on a throne, waiting for me to mess up so He could "zap" me! Sadly, it filtered into my adult life, and even into my marriage, causing me to even fear the most gentle, loving, understanding and supportive person in my life; my husband. Yet, even though I lived in fear every day, I didn't need to.

How hurtful do you think it is to someone to know that, while they love you for who you are, you are still afraid of them and are intimidated by them? How do you think the Lord feels?

Until the Lord finally healed me of the years of oppression and hurt that I was packing deep within me, I lived in a constant state of indecision, confusion, and fear. None of that is of God. None. Of. It.

Be encouraged today; if the Lord has given you a task, don't sit and work yourself up into a tizzy in fear. The enemy would like nothing better than for you to get so afraid that you chicken out before you can complete your task. Therefore, here's my encouragement: DO IT AFRAID! If you do, I promise you the Lord will meet you as soon as you take the first step in faith and help you continue moving forward!

Lights for Your Path

1 Corinthians 14:33
Joshua 1:9
Deuteronomy 31:8

Day 13

Get Grounded and Move Forward

But if we are living in the light, as God is in the light, then we have fellowship with each other, and the blood of Jesus, his Son, cleanses us from all sin. ~1 John 1:7

When God heals you of an issue, or several issues, that you've had buried deep within your soul, you come out of it into a new light. At first it's hard to see things around you because it's so bright and clear out in the open. But gradually things begin to adjust. You're at a sort of standstill because there's a newness within you; a getting-used-to-this-new-life kind of feeling. It takes a little getting used to. There's a new awareness. Peace, joy, happiness, and laughter all come back to you.

There can also be remembered hurts. There

are those little aggravating voices, trying to sprout old hurts back into life. But instantly, they are squashed back into the pit from whence they came. There is no more dwelling on the issues of the past because, let's face it, they are in the past. It's a new day and you're a new you!

Therefore, what happens when you finally adjust somewhat and the newness wears off? That's when the moving forward begins. Taking those baby steps, walking steps, then running steps forward. Get grounded by staying in prayer. Keep reading your Bible. This will help you move forward and will keep you grounded.

We have to move forward in our journey if we are to be successful. If we stay where we are, we end up going backwards. No one wants to end up back in the black hole, yet there are also people who try to keep us from moving forward. So beware on the path!

Let me encourage you today. Let God ground you in His presence, in His Word, in His conversation, in everything. Let Him light your path. When you get grounded in Him, you'll be able to move forward with confidence and ease.

Lights for Your Path

Joshua 1:8
Psalm 1:2
Colossians 4:2
Psalm 119:11

Day 14
Walking in the Fog

If we confess our sins, He is faithful and just to forgive us our sins and to cleanse us from all unrighteousness.
~1 John 1:9 (NKJV)

Walking this healing path, sometimes we will run into fog. It happens. We may wake up one morning, begin our daily walk, and there seems to be fog not only on our physical path, but even in our heart, our brain, our spirit. Being encompassed in fog, the scenery can be eerie, ethereal, and yet, intimidating all at the same time; the beauty of the scenery around us hidden from view. However, God is still in control. He is in charge of everything in and around us, even in the fog.

On our spiritual walk though, if we don't pay attention on our life's path, we can become quite foggy. We get so caught up in the things we need to do that we take our eyes off Jesus; therefore the fog descends and blocks our spiritual vision. We lose our focus. We don't read our Bible. We may even begin to allow thoughts and feelings pop into our head that really have no business being there. It's amazing to me how one simple thought can lead to another, then another, and before long the fog is so thick that you can't find your way out! It's a scary place to be when you're surrounded by fog and can't see your surroundings.

Something we need to remember; keep your eyes focused on God, and He will keep His eyes on you.

When you have taken your eyes off Him, fortunately there is a solution; a very quick, very distinct solution. Take a deep breath, spread your hands in surrender, and begin praying. Within a few words, you will begin to feel that sweet peace come over you and you'll begin to relax. The fog will lift, not only in your heart, but on the path as well and you'll begin to see both physically and spiritually.

One time when I was literally standing in fog, I began praying and my fog began to lift; within and around me. As it did, I noticed two little birds that had been sitting on the fence posts. They had been there, but I hadn't been able to see them. Now I could. As I watched them watching me, I felt as if they were there to reassure me that not only does He take care of them, but He wants me to know He's taking care of me, too. How much more valuable I am than they, and they are so precious!

You are precious to Him, too. If you'll take your fogginess to Him, He will begin to gently blow it away and before long, you'll be able to see on the path once more.

Lights for Your Path

Matthew 6:26
2 Corinthians 3:16
Proverbs 4:25
Deuteronomy 7:6

Day 15

Play in the Rain

You visit the earth and water it, You greatly enrich it; The river of God is full of water; You provide their grain, For so You have prepared it.
~Psalm 65:9 (NKJV)

Some days, it rains. Yet, it's often necessary for a little cleansing, and healing, to wash away dirt, and impurities. It also settles the dust around us so we can have a clean, clear path in which to walk. There is such a beautiful scent after a rain. The air just smells so pure. Wouldn't you agree?

It's refreshing to stand, barefoot, in a cool puddle on the walkway, or porch, look out over the area and see how the rain cleaned and healed the trees, grass, flowers, and well, everything. Healing rain. We all need some of that once in a while.

I once experienced this myself after a round of thunderstorms went through our area. I had been feeling beat down and felt spiritually and emotionally a mess. Standing, looking out over our property, I began to lift my voice to the Lord, reading aloud from the Psalms. Proclaiming God's Word out loud, His promises over me, I suddenly knew He was letting me know He heard me. He began to lift me up and calm me.

God knows all that you've been going through, too. He hasn't given up on you. He wants you to know He has something for you to do, but you must trust Him. You must bring everything within you to Him and give it to Him. Just be honest; with yourself and with God.

Today, I want to encourage you to look up Psalm 25 and read verses one through seven, out loud. Let God's love wash over you and refresh you. Throw down your umbrella and come play in the rain! God's healing rain!

Lights for Your Path

Psalm 25:1-7
Job 5:10
Psalm 68:9
Job 36:28
Joel 2:23

Day 16

Frustration on the Path

The Lord isn't really being slow about his promise, as some people think. No, he is being patient for your sake. He does not want anyone to be destroyed, but wants everyone to repent.
~2 Peter 3:9

Life can be full of frustrations. They can come in many forms, whether it's your family, job, financial, spiritual, physical, mental or even emotional. We face frustration every day of our lives. When we do, it can be very easy to get an attitude of frustration and begin to gripe and grumble.

I got frustrated one day simply trying to fold a fitted sheet. Can I get an amen? I mean, the flat sheet and even pillow cases folded nice and flat. But, when I got to that fitted sheet, all bets were off. That thing just would not fold the way I wanted it to. I became frustrated. I may have ended up wadding it up and stuffing it into the closet so I couldn't see it. Lumpy and bumpy.

You know, that's how some people become when they're frustrated; lumpy and bumpy, griping and grumbling. Yet, even in that emotional state we are still useful to God. We still have a purpose, He still loves us, and His plan for us never changes.

However, even though we may have frustration on our healing path, God is so full of love and mercy and He is always ready and willing to pour that out to us. He longs to give us our heart's desire. Regardless if we're smooth and mellow, like a flat sheet, or if we're lumpy and bumpy like a fitted sheet. We all have a purpose. We all have a function. There is a place for you in God's big sheet set. He can take you, fold you, smooth out the creases, lumps and bumps, and make you something quite beautiful. You just have to let Him.

Lights for Your Path

Philippians 2:14
Jeremiah 29:11
1 Corinthians 12:12

Day 17

Come Out of the Cave

Brenda West

I pour out my complaints before him and tell him all my troubles. When I am overwhelmed, you alone know the way I should turn. ~Psalm 142:2-3a

Do you ever just feel like hiding? I think we all do once in a while. In Psalm 142, David is pouring out his troubles to God while taking refuge in a cave from his enemies. You may not be hiding in a cave, and perhaps your enemy isn't someone physical, but rather loneliness, despair, rejection, or grief. Although your situation is different from David's, you can follow his example and cry out to God just the same.

As David poured out his troubles to God, we can be assured that we, too, can tell God everything. He is the Best Listener. Don't be afraid to cry out to God. He can take it. He hears us in our time of weeping and helps us in our distress. The last thing He wants us to do is hide.

David had been hiding in a cave to avoid the traps set by his enemy, King Saul. However, David didn't stay in the cave. He reminded himself of God's faithfulness and that God's ways are always perfect. He didn't allow the enemy to steal his destiny or identity of being King David to God's people.

Is your trap, which is set by the enemy, one of depression, self-pity, fear, doubt, or grief? Be like David and come out of your cave. Don't continue to hide, allowing the enemy to rob you of your identity and lose your destiny. Trust and believe God's promises. He has wonderful, great big plans for you.

Lights for Your Path

Psalm 142
Jeremiah 29:11

Day 18
A Fork in the Path

"Enter by the narrow gate…" ~Matthew 7:13 (NKJV)

Have you ever tried following directions someone gave you, only to discover a fork in the road that you weren't warned about? I can totally identify with that. A while back, I was trying to find my way to a job site my husband and son were working at. As contractors, they sometimes need something extra, or something that didn't get picked up for the last delivery. Therefore, it often falls to me to bring it to them.

I had been given what I thought were clear directions; at least, until I got to "the fork in the road." Then, I couldn't remember which direction I was supposed to go; right or left. I went left. The road became gravel, got narrow, and I suddenly realized I wasn't where I was supposed to be. At least, I thought I wasn't because there was another fork in the road. I went left again. Wrong.

I decided to call for a refresher in directions. Yet, I had no signal. I tried anyway. Fortunately, my husband answered and it turns out I was right where I was supposed to be, the only exception was I turned the wrong way at the last fork. That fork turned out to be the driveway I was supposed to turn into. However, I wasn't given that information. As I came up that driveway, I looked up and saw my son, standing on the roof of the house, waving. I was there the whole time and thought I was lost.

Many times we take the road everyone else is on, never knowing a whole other world of beauty is out there, if we had only taken the narrow road.

Jesus teaches that in order to get to Him, we have to take the narrow path. The gate that not many are entering through is the one that will allow us to see His face. In today's society, following the "norm" is what's popular. If we don't, we are generally shunned, not only by the general public, but often by our own Christian brothers and sisters. Sadly, many have forgotten that being a true follower of Christ means being a sold-out believer and taking the narrow, not-so-used path.

Which path are you on? May I suggest taking the narrow path at the fork?

Lights for Your Path

Matthew 7:13-14
Proverbs 2:20
Proverbs 4:14
Proverbs 14:2

Day 19
Don't Look Back!

But one thing I do: Forgetting what is behind and straining toward what is ahead...
~Philippians 3:13 (NKJV)

Have you ever had Rear-View Mirror Syndrome? I guess it could be compared to Rubber-Necking, except they're kind of the same thing; looking backwards as you're moving forward.

You've seen it, or done it, I'm sure. Let there be an accident on the highway, or you see a police officer pull someone over. Or maybe you're driving through town and catch a glimpse of something interesting in a store front window. That's when you turn and look all while continuing to drive forward. It's all fine and dandy until you, yourself, crash into something for not watching where you're going.

It's the same in life situations.

I had this problem. I was always looking back

on what I could have done better, what I should have done better, how I could have, should have, and didn't avoid mishaps in my life. I had a lot of regrets. Can you identify? The difference now than then is that I have learned the way to get over Rear-View Mirror Syndrome.

It all comes down to forgiveness. We know that God forgives us, but what we often fail to recognize is that when He forgives, He forgets! Yet, the saddest thing is we don't forgive or forget, not only with others, but especially when it comes to ourselves. We maintain Rear-View Mirror Syndrome, always looking back. Sadder still are those who simply will not let anything go.

You know, watching reruns of things in the past doesn't give you a true picture. Think about it. Everything in the rear-view mirror is backwards, obscure, and it tends to get a bit foggy. Most people neglect to read the writing on the mirror before looking: "Objects in mirror are closer than they appear." Sometimes, looking back into the rear-view mirror, bringing up things in the past, can cause a lot of arguments and hurts, when it's better left alone. In looking back, those things are distorted more and more until it no longer looks like it did when it happened, possibly years ago.

Forgiveness; the best remedy for Rear-View Mirror Syndrome.

Lights for Your Path

Philippians 3:14-15
Hebrews 12:15
1 Timothy 6:11

Day 20
Setbacks, Struggles, and Stress

The God of peace will soon crush Satan under your feet. The grace of our Lord Jesus be with you.
~Romans 16:20 (NKJV)

Part of this journey on life's healing path is that we have setbacks. We have struggles. Things and people cause us stress. But we must decide to rise above it, to not allow these things to dictate our lives. What am I talking about? Basically everything!

I've had many setbacks in my life. One particular memory was the day I thought I was having a heart attack. Let me just say that, when you make a conscious decision to serve the LORD, to rise up and walk out the calling He has placed on your life, the enemy, the devil, will begin attacking you with everything he knows will cause you issues. Now, let me follow that up with, DO NOT LET HIM! Don't believe his lies, and they are lies. Don't let him convince you there's something wrong with you, when you know in truth, there is not.

When we break generational curses over our lives and the lives of our family, the devil loses in a big way. It makes him mad. So, of course, he is going to attack more. But if you're like me and enjoy looking at the humorous side of things, read on: The devil has already lost and we are declared winners, by the blood of Jesus Christ!

Therefore, the morning I was attacked with chest pain, my husband came rushing home at my call to him regarding what was going on. When he walked in the door, saw me crying, he reminded me, ever so lovingly, of some events that had been going on in our lives. With that, my light bulb came on and I felt very foolish. I had been neglecting some very important things in my life, including prayer.

When we get too confident and begin to neglect our prayer time, our Bible-reading time, and let our minds wander to things not of God, the enemy will sneak in and attack us in our weakened state. If we aren't prepared (which at this point, we won't be) we will fall for his lies and our lives will become set back, we will begin to struggle and we will have stress.

But it doesn't have to be that way.

We can nip it in the bud immediately by going straight to our Source of peace; Jesus. Remember, dear ones, Jesus is our Peace, our Confidence, our Hope, our Healer, and our very essence of life. He is our Partner along this path, this journey. Prevent setbacks, struggles, and stress in your life by staying in contact with the One who will guide you always.

Lights for Your Path

Romans 16:20
1 John 1:9
1 Peter 5:8

Day 21
Focus!

...looking unto Jesus, the author and finisher of our faith... ~Hebrews 12:2a (NKJV)

My husband and I used to love riding motorcycles. We loved the freedom we felt as we would ride down the road, wind blowing all around us. Truthfully, we loved riding in the mountains of North Carolina along the Blue Ridge Parkway. Leaning into the twists and turns was refreshing and exciting all at the same time. Plus, the scenery is absolutely beautiful.

While enjoying being in the mountains, we also know it's very important to stay focused on where we are going if we want to stay on the mountain road. One wrong turn of the head, especially on a motorcycle, can send a person plummeting off the side of the cliff. What I mean is, on a motorcycle, whichever way you look, that is where you will go.

You know, when we begin to watch the

scenery around us instead of watching God, we can end up the same way. We can skid on the pathway and ultimately go over a cliff. There are many things in this world that can cause us to lose our focus. Many of them are things we don't even realize can make us slip! But, when we put our eyes on Jesus, He will give us more beautiful scenery than we could ever find anywhere else.

Where is your focus today? Are you watching where you're going? Or are you watching everything else around you? Here's a challenge for you today: Keep your focus on Jesus. Let Him guide you on this path and see the marvelous, wonderful things He can show you.

Lights for Your Path

Hebrews 12:1-2
Joshua 1:8
Luke 11:28

Day 22

When the Waters Rise

When you go through deep waters, I will be with you. ~Isaiah 43:2a

As I write this today, it's raining. There's an old saying that goes, "April showers bring May flowers." I don't mind so much, really. At least, I don't until we have so much rain that our field begins to flood, which happens quite often with a lot of rainfall. However, one year, it flooded so badly our house flooded, and we ultimately lost the entire house.

I'm reminded of the times when depression would overtake me. It felt like a flood that I couldn't stop. When engulfed in the black hole of it, I felt as if I were drowning. Rather, I felt as if I were going to drown.

That's probably how the Disciples felt when they were in a boat in the middle of a storm. The winds came up and the waters began churning and sloshing over the sides of the vessel. Where was

Jesus? Asleep! How could He possibly sleep in the middle of a storm on the sea, with waves crashing all around and over the sides of the boat? Yet, He was. He wasn't worried at all. However, the Disciples were.

Isn't that how we are today? When storms of life come crashing down and the waters of depression, anxiety, panic, intimidation, fear, or whatever it is that gets to you begin to rise, that's when you need to call out to Jesus. Declare your victory over the rising waters. They may swirl and crash all around you, but they won't overtake you. Because, you have Jesus as your Life Saver. Even if He doesn't calm the waters, He will calm you, His child.

As flood waters will eventually go back down, whatever waters you're riding will also go back down. When you see them rising, have faith. Smile and look up! Jesus knows exactly where you are, and He has everything under control. No need to worry!

Lights for Your Path

Matthew 8:23-25
Matthew 8:26
Philippians 4:6-7
Isaiah 43:2

Day 23

Encouragement Along the Path

Kerri Taylor

Let us think of ways to motivate one another to acts of love and good works. ~Hebrews 10:24

When I think about encouragement, or being encouraged, I think about cheering for my high school football team. Our cheerleading squad would always encourage our football team, helping them to believe they could win the game, and to keep moving forward. I especially loved when we would cheer our team on with only a few minutes left in the game, encouraging them to keep pushing through. Even if they would not make the touchdown, our cheerleading squad would keep cheering for them to keep working for the next touchdown.

That's the way it is in our walk on the healing

path. We must keep moving forward. We must keep cheering each other on, to press through each trial, each struggle, each stage in our walk. Find that one sister or brother in Christ and motivate them; You can do it!

You've got this!
Keep moving forward!
Press through!
Don't give up!
God's got you!
Keep going!

It's important to have a walking buddy. With every step we take on this journey, we need each other daily, to help encourage and spur each other on. But the greatest Walking Buddy we could have is Jesus. He promised that He would always be with us, through every trial, every struggle, and that He would never leave us.

Jesus never said we wouldn't have struggles. However, He did say He would walk with us through them. Whatever you're going through today, be encouraged. This will pass. You won't be overtaken. You will get through it, because you are more than victorious, through Jesus Christ!

Lights for Your Path

Psalm 23:2-4
Hebrews 10:24
1 Thessalonians 5:11
1 Corinthians 14:3

Day 24

Running on the Path

You were running the race so well. Who has held you back from following the truth? ~Galatians 5:7

Have you ever felt as if you've been running, but haven't got anywhere? I felt that way once. It seemed as if I had been running and didn't know it. I didn't go anywhere. I just hadn't paid attention like I should. Oddly enough, I felt as if something changed, but I couldn't put my finger on what.

Reading the blog of a friend one day put things into perspective for me. I realized I hadn't been to The Stoop (the spot on my porch where I pray) in a while. It had been so cold in the mornings that I hadn't ventured outside to my porch, to stand and talk to the Lord.

I get into these little funks from time to time. I shy away from prayer like it is the plague. I begin to feel as if I'm bothering God because I seem to say the same things every time I talk to Him.

Doesn't He get tired of hearing it? I begin to feel as if I'm not a productive pray-er, so-to-speak. Which couldn't be further from the truth.

On her blog, my friend told of how she experienced friend a "soul quenching" one night when she walked out into her orchard to find her lost dog. She then realized how beautiful, quiet, and soul quenching it was. She could see the stars, feel the breeze, and just felt peaceful and in the presence of the Lord. Reading it, I felt jealous! I couldn't believe it.

That's when I received a little prompting, reminding me I hadn't been out on The Stoop and I hadn't made the effort to come talk to the Lord. Where was God through all this? Waiting. He had been waiting for me to get my act together and figure myself out. He's never been pushy. He's never been derogatory. He's never even made me talk to Him. It's just that I always feel bad when I don't. Can you relate?

The best part about all of this is that, even though I flit from time to time, God never leaves me. He understands me. He loves me. He waits for me. And never, I mean never does he throw my mistakes back at me. I never have to worry or be afraid. Yes, I mess up. But when I come to Him, He's there, ready to listen. Ready to comfort. Ready to love me, just as always.

He's there for you, too, my friend. Waiting.

Watching. Listening. As He has always promised He would do. Try Him and see for yourself.

Lights for Your Path

Psalm 34:4
Deuteronomy 4:31
Colossians 4:2

Day 25

Stuck in a Rut

And we know [with great confidence] that God [who is deeply concerned about us] causes all things to work together [as a plan] for good for those who love God, to those who are called according to His plan and purpose. ~Romans 8:28 (ABNT)

There are many things going on in the world today. Many people running this way and that, trying to figure out the meaning of life. Many people are trying to figure out the where's and why's, working themselves from sun up to sundown to have a successful career, busy, busy, busy. They're stuck in a rut and probably don't even know it.

You may be stuck in that rut today. Whatever it is, whether from work, school, home, or maybe it isn't any of those but the circumstances you find yourself in. Maybe it's depression, addiction, abuse, anxiety, finances, or something else. May I encourage you today? You won't be there for long. It might seem like a lifetime to you, but rest assured it is but a moment to God. He is working something wonderful for you. However, it is up to you to hang in there and trust Him. It also helps to cry out to Him. He is always there, listening, watching, waiting.

God knows every single event of your life; every single tear you have shed, every sigh, every thought, everything. He knows the way out of that rut and He will use every negative thing in your life to make something good out of it, and maybe just teach you a few things in the process! I know this from experience.

I've been broken and bruised mentally, emotionally, physically, and spiritually. Yet, while it wasn't easy going through the things I did, I thought I would never get out of that rut. But I did! You can, too!

When we are in a mess, all we have to do is ask. Call out to the LORD and He is there, ready to help us out of that rut, out of each and every situation we are in. The only problem is that we usually never think to ask God.

Jesus is the only way out of the rut you're in. Why not stop now and ask Him for help? I'll be you'll be surprised how fast He answers you.

Lights for Your Path

Psalm 56:3-4
Psalm 56:8

Day 26

Get Up!

The LORD gave this message to Jonah son of Amittai: "Get up and go to the great city of Nineveh." ~Jonah 1:1a

When God told Jonah to go to Nineveh… he ran. He didn't just run. He ran in the opposite direction! Jonah did not do what God told him to do. He didn't want to, at first. How often have I been guilty of that very same thing? Sadly, too many times.

Often we have that little hint of an idea we need to do something important. Go see a certain person. Take a meal to someone. Encourage someone. But we hesitate. We second-guess. Ultimately, we talk ourselves out of doing what we know in our hearts we should have done. Then, we feel guilt, remorse, shame, all the things the enemy loves to throw at us for not being obedient.

If that's you today, if you have that little unction you need to do something, let me encourage you: Get Up! Go do it. Even if you get up with a bad attitude just know that your attitude will not stop a move of God. His plans will always be accomplished, bad attitude or not. Nothing or no one will get in His way.

Jonah didn't get up and go. He went opposite and with a bad attitude and well, we all know what happened to him! I'll just tell you, I don't fancy being swallowed by a great fish and having to spend three days in its belly, pondering my actions. However, even after three days, when the fish spit Jonah out onto dry ground, he was exactly where God had told him to go in the first place! In my mind, if I don't go where God tells me, He will get me there any way He can. Might as well just do it.

This journey we are on is full of surprises. We are often presented with things we don't want to do, or things that are unpleasant. But if we take ourselves and our feelings out of the situation and focus on what God is trying to accomplish, we might just learn something, and the blessing will be tremendous.

Of course, it's not about getting a blessing, but rather about being obedient to what the Holy Spirit tells you to do. It doesn't always go smoothly, nor does it always turn out for the good. Many times people are given the Word from God and they don't listen. They don't turn to Him. Eventually it catches up with them. Don't be one of those.

When you know God has given you a message, or an order, Get UP! Go! Do what you've been commissioned to do. I guarantee you will feel a whole lot better. Things may not work out as you had hoped, but at least. You did what God told you to. That's all you are required to do. Be obedient. God will take care of the rest, and you. It's a promise.

Lights for Your Path

Isaiah 55:11
Jonah 3:1-5
Jeremiah 7:23

Day 27
Rescue on the Path

"And whatever things you ask in prayer, believing, you will receive." ~Matthew 21:22 (NKJV)

When God healed me, He literally fixed me from the inside out. I didn't have to rely on someone else to pour out my troubles to, to give me justification, pity, acceptance, or anything else to make me feel better. When God healed me, He gave me all those things and more. Not only that, but when God healed me, He turned me around and gently nudged me in this direction, toward you.

My assignment, if you will, is to give you hope. It's to tell you what God has done for me and that He wants to heal you, too. He wants me to send you His way. In fact, I'll walk with you. That's why we are on this path, dear ones, because just up ahead, God is waiting for you. There is rescue on this path!

Sometimes it's a little scary to be on a new

path. You don't know the exact way to go. It helps to have a guide, a friend, someone who can lead you in the right direction. Where you find rescue depends on how far you want to travel. Your rescue may happen right away. It may take a bit further on the path. What I mean by that is, some are ready for the healing, others are not.

There are twists and turns on the path, detours, bumps, potholes, and side paths that lead nowhere. I've been on them myself. While some of them are not fun, they have proven to be a learning experience that I now cherish because they helped me to grow in my healing walk. You will find that, too.

The enemy will try to blindside us on this path. Don't let him. He will also send broken and hurting people onto the path who may not be ready to walk healed. My experience is that hurting people hurt people. But rescued people rescue people. If you find rescue on the path, you can help rescue people. Help them walk healed. Love them. Nurture them. Be patient with them. But whatever you do, don't enable them to stay hurt.

This pathway of healing is a long one, but oh, so rewarding! We will enjoy small victories and rewards along the way and one day we will receive the "Big Reward" – eternity in Heaven with Jesus!

Lights for Your Path

2 Corinthians 1:10
Psalm 18:27
Psalm 119:170

Day 28
Far Out!

"The Spirit of the LORD is upon me, for he has anointed me to bring Good News to the poor. He has sent me to proclaim that captives will be released, that the blind will see that the oppressed will be set free, and that the time of the LORD's favor has come." ~Luke 4:18-19

Sometimes, God gives us some far-out assignments. Some of His promises are way out there and well, they just seem too far-out to comprehend, or believe. Do you agree?

I mean, look at Abraham and Sarah, Gideon, Zechariah, Elizabeth, and even Mary (Jesus' mother). Maybe you, yourself, have been given an assignment and you think, wow that's just far out, God! I understand.

When God healed me, He gave me an assignment, too. A promise. He told me, through a very godly man, first that He would heal me, and second, that I would minister to women and give them encouragement and hope. My initial thought was, "Oh, God, not them!" But God's answer was, "Yes! Them."

Women were the ones who intimidated me the most. Many of them were the ones who hurt me the worst, who kept me in misery, who judged me the harshest. Yet, they are the exact ones God sent me back into the ring to fight for. What a far-out promise. What a far-out task!

Each one of the above-mentioned people received a far-out promise from God... including me. Each far-out promise was backed up and fulfilled. God is in the promise making and promise keeping business. He never breaks a promise. He never goes back on His word. You can bet, if He told you to do something, and that you will do something, it will happen!

When God healed me, I never dreamed that what I would be doing would be ministering to the very people who intimidated me the most. Yet, here I am. I also get to meet many more women who are broken and hurting just like I was, and God opens the door to allow me to tell them there is hope for them.

What good would my healing be if I never shared it with others? What good would yours be if you never shared it? Healed people help hurting people find hope and healing through the capable hands of Jesus. This is my calling. It's what I do.

I'm not a counselor, though some think I am. I'm just one of the called.

What if we all took our far-out assignments today and used them to bring hope and healing to someone?

That would really be Far Out!

Lights for Your Path

Genesis 18:1-15
Judges 6:33-40
Luke 1:5-23
Luke 1:26-38

Day 29
Truth is Greater than Fact

Jesus told him, "I am the way, the truth, and the life. No one can come to the Father except through me."
~John 14:6

So often today people jump to conclusions before they get the truth. Too many times the conclusion is drawn even before they know the back story of the one whom they are jumping to conclusions about. We see this all over the news and social media every day. Although it could all be avoided with just a little less talking and a whole lot of listening and praying.

In society today, it seems people would rather believe anything than the truth. But truth is greater than fact. The fact is, there will always be someone, somewhere who doesn't like you, or me, or anyone else, for some reason known only to them. The truth is, God loves us all the time and He is greater than all.

The fact is, people will condemn you for things you did in your past, whether you were at fault or not. The truth is, God does not condemn you.

The fact is, people will refuse to forgive you for anything and everything, regardless of how many times you say you are sorry. The truth is, once you ask God for forgiveness, you're forgiven, and God forgets it.

The fact is, people will tell you they received their information "from a reliable source." The truth is, there is no such thing in society. God is your only reliable source.

You belong to the Most-High God, not society, not to other people. You especially don't belong to those whom you are friends with. You belong to God.

God's Word is the first Word, and the last Word, on who you are. Jesus is that Word. He loves you. He is crazy about you. He wants to give you the best life you can possibly have. So stop jumping to conclusions and stop listening to other jumpers. Get the Truth, because Truth is greater than fact.

Lights for Your Path

James 1:19
Psalm 136:1
Romans 8:1
1 John 1:9
Psalm 119:114
Galatians 3:9; 4:7

Day 30
Continue the Journey

He reached down and drew me from the deep, dark hole where I was stranded, mired in the muck and clay. With a gentle hand, He pulled me out To set me down safely on a warm rock; He held me until I was steady enough to continue the journey again. ~Psalm 40:2 (The Voice)

The more I walk the path with God, the more I learn. The more I learn, the more clarity I have spiritually, mentally, and emotionally.

In my clarity one thing that has been made very clear is that I do have enemies on this journey. One in particular hates me more than anything in this world. For years, I have heard that I need to be alert, I need to pay attention, because that great enemy is prowling around like a roaring lion, looking for someone to devour.

One day I actually had a bit of a revelation: though my enemy roars like a lion, he can do me no harm. It's almost as if he's toothless. Oh, he may prowl, roar, intimidate, strike at me and possibly knock me off the path a bit. He may knock me down into the mud, or a hole. But I won't stay there. Neither will you, dear one.

Yes, we have setbacks and struggles. But they don't have to be permanent. You don't have to repeat the same things over and over again. You don't have to stay stranded or stuck.

The day you decide enough is enough and become willing to allow Him to help you, will be the day God re-routes your journey. Reach up! Because, that will be the day God reaches down, pulls you out of the deep, dark hole where you're mired in the muck, and sets you on a warm rock. He will hold you and steady you until you are steady enough to continue your journey.

Lights for Your Path

1 Peter 5:8
John 10:10

About the Author

Shelley Wilburn was born and raised in West Frankfort, Illinois. She began writing when she was twelve years old. At present, Shelley has authored four books, written several articles and devotions for various newspapers, women's magazines and newsletters, and also co-authored devotionals. In addition to writing, Shelley is also an avid reader, book reviewer, blogger, and speaker. She is the founder, and president, of Walking Healed Ministries LTD which helps people who struggle with depression and anxiety to find healing and wholeness through Jesus Christ. Using her love of writing, and wearing mismatched socks, Shelley has developed a unique ministry of encouraging others using biblical truths and stories from her own personal life. Shelley and her husband D.A. are the parents of three grown children and make their home in West Frankfort, Illinois. Together, they have been in ministry since 2000.

About Walking Healed Ministries LTD

Walking Healed Ministries (aka WHM) was founded by Shelley Wilburn after her miraculous healing, in 2012, from depression and anxiety. She began writing and blogging full-time, on her own website and making guest appearances on the blogs of other authors. By sharing her writing on social media, Shelley began to see a need for encouragement and healing, in the responses to her posts from others. Within a few short years of her healing she had published her first book, and realized, surprisingly, that Walking Healed Ministries had been born.

Walking Healed Ministries LTD received

501(c)(3) nonprofit organization and public charity ministry status in February 2019, which made this important ministry legal and official. WHM was organized for, and is dedicated to, helping people find healing from depression, anxiety, intimidation, and the things which keep them from achieving the abundant life Jesus came to give them.

Those associated with Walking Healed Ministries seek to inspire and empower people to walk their daily lives healed and whole. Dedicated to being uplifting and encouraging to all, their goal is for people to discover who they are in Christ, and to confidently go out and do likewise.

There are many free resources and downloads available at Walking Healed Ministries, with new ones being added frequently. Please visit the online store for more information to help you with your spiritual needs by visiting

https://shelleywilburn.org/index.php/store.

You can also read more information about Walking Healed Ministries LTD, Shelley Wilburn's healing testimony, and read encouragement from blog posts by visiting

https://walkinghealed.org.

To contact the author write:
Walking Healed Ministries LTD
3398 Deering Rd.
West Frankfort, IL 62896

Internet Address: www.walkinghealed.org

Please include your testimony of help received from this book when you write. Your prayer requests are welcome.

Follow the author at the following social media outlets:
Facebook:
www.facebook.com/authorshelleywilburn
Instagram:
www.instagram.com/shelleywilburn
Pinterest:
www.pinterest.com/shelleyawilburn

Other Books by Shelley Wilburn

Walking Healed, A Journey of Forgiveness, Grace, and Hope

Written in diary form, Shelley Wilburn's book, Walking Healed, is her journey after being healed of over forty years of mental and emotional issues including depression, anxiety, and intimidation. Using snippets of her healing journey along with biblical truths, Shelley takes the reader on a journey of healing, forgiveness, grace and hope, then leads into finding your purpose.

Written for those who suffer the pain and loneliness of depression and intimidation, Shelley reaches down in the black hole, finds those who are hurting and helps them find their way out.

Walking Healed will help the reader realize that even Christians suffer depression. Shelley Wilburn knows and understands this from her personal experience with depression and anxiety. She also knows the freedom from these issues when God heals you and takes you on a wonderful journey of walking healed. Shelley's story of healing helps others know that even depression is curable and "nothing is impossible with God."

Walking Healed Companion Study

As a companion to *Walking Healed*, the *Walking Healed Companion Bible Study* is a five-week journey into discovering healing, forgiveness, grace, hope, and finding your purpose. Designed to be used in conjunction with the *Walking Healed* book, Shelley Wilburn leads you into the depths of the Bible to discover healing for whatever holds you captive. She will then lead you in discovering forgiveness, God's grace, and the hope He gives us. The final week, you will begin to discover how all these attributes converge to help you journey to discover your purpose in life.

Walking Healed and its companion study is designed to help women (and men) break free and live the life God intended for them. A definite must read. Available wherever books are sold.

Warrior Princess: Ignite Your Inner Warrior

One of the foundational principles in life is to understand who we are and what our purpose is in this life. But often, we find ourselves floundering.

Warrior Princess is a powerful, call-to-action Bible study, with journal and coloring pages tucked within the eight-week plan, that takes you on an interactive journey to discover your identity according to God's Word. Designed to awaken the inner warrior within the depths of your soul *Warrior Princess* will help you discover that you were chosen, and planned for, even before the foundations of the world, and what it truly means to be a daughter of the Most-High God.

O Mighty Warrior: Igniting the Warrior Within

Do you know who you are?

One of the most important foundational principles in a man's life is to know and understand who you are and what your purpose is.

Many men today don't seem to realize they have spiritual authority to do the things God has called them to do. *O Mighty Warrior* is a powerful call-to-action journey. It's a call to stand in your spiritual authority as men, spiritual leaders of your home, igniting the warrior within the depths of your soul.

O Mighty Warrior will help you discover that Warrior you were chosen to be even before the foundations of the world.

You can find all these titles, apparel, and resources for your journey, on the Walking Healed Ministries online store. Just go to http://shelleywilburn.org/index.php/store/

www.ingramcontent.com/pod-product-compliance
Lightning Source LLC
Chambersburg PA
CBHW030604020526
44112CB00048B/1210